What Is the Godzilla?

by Sheila Keenan

illustrated by Robert Squier

Penguin Workshop

For Bruce, King of the Friends—SK

For the biggest Godzilla fan I've ever known:
eight-year-old me, who would have happily drawn
all these pictures for the fun of it—RS

PENGUIN WORKSHOP
An imprint of Penguin Random House LLC, New York

First published in the United States of America by Penguin Workshop,
an imprint of Penguin Random House LLC, New York, 2024

TM & © TOHO CO., LTD.

PENGUIN is a registered trademark and PENGUIN WORKSHOP is a trademark
of Penguin Books Ltd. WHO HQ & Design is a registered trademark
of Penguin Random House LLC.

Visit us online at penguinrandomhouse.com.

Library of Congress Cataloging-in-Publication Data is available.

Printed in the United States of America

ISBN 9780593658482 (paperback)   10 9 8 7 6 5 4 3 2 1 CJKW
ISBN 9780593658499 (library binding)   10 9 8 7 6 5 4 3 2 1 CJKW

Contents

What Is the Story of Godzilla? 1

The Monster Awakens 6

Go, Gojira! 12

How Did They Do That? 26

Headed to America 43

Emperor Eras 50

Big, Bad, and Back 63

Millennium Era Onward 74

High Tech in Hollywood *and* Tokyo 84

Living Legend 100

Bibliography 106

What Is the Story of Godzilla?

On October 10, 2020, government officials and other notable people stood on a red platform decorated with ribbon in Nijigen no Mori (say: NEE-jee-gen no MO-ree) Park on Awaji Island, Japan. After a few short speeches, smoke suddenly billowed out from several cannons. A deafening roar filled the air. The officials cut the ribbon.

Behind them a few brave people whooshed by on a zip line headed directly into the gaping, jagged-toothed mouth of an enormous monster, 180 feet long and 75 feet high.

Its giant eyes glared and its inner belly glowed.

The world's first Godzilla theme park attraction was now open!

Officially named "Godzilla Interception Operation Awaji," it celebrates one of the most famous monsters in the world.

The beast first came to life in 1954 in a movie created, directed, and produced in Japan. Since then, it has appeared in dozens of movies and other media.

The monster is known to millions for its thundering footsteps, frightening cry, and blazing heat-ray breath. Audiences fear or cheer Godzilla, because sometimes the supersize prehistoric beast is the enemy of humankind, and sometimes it is its friend. Either way, there's a lot of action and foot-stomping demolition involved. Godzilla has tromped through eleven Japanese locations, especially Tokyo (twelve times!). It's terrorized international cities such as New York, Boston, San Francisco, Honolulu, Beijing, and Hong Kong. No matter what language the people scurrying for cover are screaming, the monster uproar is global.

A family posing at Nijigen no Mori

Flattened buildings, squashed cars, smashed bridges, and upended trains: Godzilla leaves a huge footprint!

November 3 is called "Godzilla Day" because that's the date the first film was released in 1954. In the seven decades since then, Godzilla has become a monster record-breaker. It is the longest continuously running film franchise ever.

How Godzilla became King of the Monsters is an interesting story. It involves military history, Japanese culture, film technology, and the growing popularity of science-fiction movies. And this story starts at the dawn of a new age.

CHAPTER 1
The Monster Awakens

In 1954, when the first Godzilla movie appeared, World War II was a fresh and awful memory for many people. This widespread war

had only ended nine years earlier, and the war's end was particularly devastating in Japan.

World War II was a global battle of Germany, Italy, and Japan (the Axis Powers) versus the United Kingdom, the Soviet Union, China, and the United States (the Allies). Other countries were invaded by, or joined forces with, the Axis or Allies, too.

In May 1945, the war waged in Europe ended, but fighting continued in the Pacific. By July, the Japanese armed forces had still not surrendered to the Allies. To end the war, the United States unleashed a powerful force never seen in the history of humankind: atomic weapons. On August 6, 1945, American aircraft dropped an atom bomb on Hiroshima, Japan. Three days later, another atom bomb was detonated in Nagasaki. The death count was shocking. Both cities were reduced to toxic, smoldering ruins. Emperor Hirohito announced Japan's surrender on August 15, 1945. World War II had ended—but the nuclear age had begun.

United States bomb testing in the Pacific Ocean in 1954 renewed people's fears of nuclear weapons. Problems with that testing triggered a worldwide anti-nuke movement to ban them. It also inspired Tomoyuki Tanaka, a producer at Toho, a major Japanese film studio.

The bombing of Hiroshima

Tomoyuki Tanaka

So did a business flight he took around the same time. Tanaka looked out the window as he flew over the Pacific and wondered what might be lurking deep down in the water below.

Tanaka had seen how popular American monster movies like *King Kong* (1933) and *The Beast from 20,000 Fathoms* (1953) were. He believed now was the time for a Japanese film of this type. Tanaka also proposed that Toho do something groundbreaking: base a movie on a monster awakened by nuclear weapons. Given Japan's experiences, this made sense. However, those very same horrible experiences could also make a movie like this controversial. Japanese audiences might be shocked to see atomic violence in a monster movie. People might not want to think about questions like what happens if scientific research is misused.

Toho was willing to take a chance. The company gave Tanaka the go-ahead. He assembled a team that would create the studio's most famous movie star: Godzilla.

CHAPTER 2
Go, Gojira!

Toho Company, Ltd. was founded in Tokyo, Japan, in 1932. Movies from this film production and distribution company involved some of the country's major directors and stars. By 1953, Toho had an international company focused on getting its movies screened outside of Japan, especially in the Americas. Because of Toho's reach and reputation, and his own skills, Tomoyuki Tanaka was able to hire an incredible group to make his monster movie, *Gojira*. *Godzilla* is the English-language name of the creature. *Gojira* is its original Japanese name, which is thought to be a combination of the Japanese words *gorira* (gorilla) and *kujira* (whale). This makes sense since the movie features a big, powerful, fantastical animal that lives underwater. (Fans would eventually start calling their favorite monster "the Big G.")

The story the writers created for the first Godzilla movie came right out of recent history. Gojira, an ancient deep-sea creature, is awakened by nuclear bomb testing deep in the Pacific Ocean. With its fiery heat ray, the monster that arises is a weapon in itself.

And Gojira is not happy about what human beings are doing! All their dangerous testing is disturbing its environment.

The 1954 *Gojira* movie opens with ships and fishing boats mysteriously destroyed after blinding flashes from the ocean. Then a fishing village is hit by a storm—and something bigger! Scientists sent to the island discover giant, radioactive footprints. Suddenly a loud bell rings throughout the village. Everyone rushes for the hills and sees an enormous dinosaur-like figure submerging into the sea. *Gojira!*

The action in the movie follows government and military attempts to stop Gojira's attacks. Underwater explosives don't seem to have any effect. Next, a tall, electrified fence is built along the coast, to protect Tokyo Bay. Gojira breaks through. It rears up to its full frightening height, opens its mouth, and shoots out a scorching heat ray. The high-wire towers of the coastal fence melt!

The Father of Monster Movies

When Tomoyuki Tanaka was a child in Kashiwara, Osaka, Japan, the movie industry was also young. The first movies he ever saw were silent films. He loved them!

Tanaka worked at Toho Film Studios for almost sixty years and rose through the ranks to become Toho's chairman. He produced more than two hundred films, including twenty-two of the studio's Godzilla movies. He was very involved in the filmmaking, from developing story ideas to marketing the movies to international audiences. In discussing how the original *Gojira* movie came to be, Tanaka once told an interviewer, "I felt like doing something big." Mission accomplished!

Japanese troops and tanks can't stop the mighty monster. Fighter planes eventually drive Gojira back into the sea. By that time Tokyo is aflame, buildings are toppled, and people are fleeing or hiding. Hospitals are filled with crying children and moaning adults. It is a frightening scene, much like recent wartime.

The main characters in the movie disagree about what to do. Japanese officials just want to wipe out the murderous monster. Paleontologist-zoologist Kyohei Yamane wants to study Gojira because the giant creature has survived powerful weapons testing. Dr. Yamane believes this research would be important and useful to the people of a nation that has experienced atomic bombings.

Kyohei Yamane

Meanwhile, Yamane's fellow scientist, the moody and mysterious Daisuke Serizawa, has developed a new terrible weapon: an Oxygen

Destroyer, which sucks out all the oxygen wherever it's used. The lack of oxygen is capable of killing everything . . . including an out-of-control, 165-foot raging reptile with heat-glowing dorsal fins and fiery breath.

Daisuke Serizawa

But despite the death and destruction Gojira has caused in Tokyo, Dr. Serizawa does not want to use the Oxygen Destroyer on Gojira. He is afraid to unleash another weapon of mass destruction in the world. He fears other scientists and nations will copy his work. More Oxygen Destroyers could mean worldwide danger and disorder.

There is also a love story within this monster movie. Dr. Yamane's daughter, Emiko, is engaged to Dr. Serizawa, but she is actually in love with someone else: Hideto Ogata, a ship captain. The young couple try to tell both Dr. Yamane and Dr. Serizawa that they want to marry. But whenever they're about to declare their love, Gojira rises up from the ocean, plows through the Japanese military, crashes through the city streets, and sets everything on fire.

Emiko Yamane and Hideto Ogata

Dr. Serizawa eventually accepts that Emiko loves Hideto. Now they have to work together to convince him to use the Oxygen Destroyer.

Oxygen Destroyer

As they plead with him in his lab, Dr. Serizawa glances at a television screen. He sees news footage of all the damage and suffering Gojira has caused. A children's choir sings a solemn prayer for help. Serizawa makes a difficult choice: He agrees to use the Oxygen Destroyer against Gojira—but he burns all his research notes so no one else will ever be able to use the deadly weapon again. Now Dr. Serizawa is the only person who knows how to build an Oxygen Destroyer. The plans for it exist solely in his head. His secret is safe as long as nobody can force him to reveal it.

In the final scenes of the movie, Dr. Yamane and Emiko watch anxiously from the crowded deck of a ship as Hideto and Dr. Serizawa dress in heavy diving suits. Then they drop into the ocean, holding the Oxygen Destroyer.

The boat and divers are linked through a radio intercom.

The two men walk along the ocean floor and surprise Gojira, who seems to be napping there. The giant creature lurches toward them, clearly threatening the human intruders. Dr. Serizawa opens the Oxygen Destroyer, which starts bubbling all around the divers and Gojira. He signals to Hideto to start rising back up to the boat. With Hideto safe, Dr. Serizawa sends a last message to the boat via the radio intercom. He wishes the young couple a happy life, pulls out a knife, and slashes through his air supply tube. He is taking the secret of the Oxygen Destroyer to the grave. And that's where Gojira is headed, too!

The monster's end is dramatic. Gojira thrashes and struggles through a wall of bubbles. It rises up, breaks through the surf, and roars loudly one more time. Gojira keels over, sinks back down, and is blasted by the Oxygen Destroyer into a huge floating skeleton. Then even the bones disappear. The horror is over . . . for now.

CHAPTER 3
How Did They Do That?

Top members of "Project G," as the *Gojira* team was called, included the movie's director and cowriter, Ishiro Honda, the special effects expert Eiji Tsuburaya, and the soundtrack composer Akira Ifukube, who also created the giant beast's signature sound.

Ishiro Honda

Ishiro Honda was an experienced filmmaker who had been drafted into the Japanese army during World War II. The war and the vivid dreams he had of it afterward affected him deeply. For Honda, the

Gojira movie was a way to promote ideas about world peace and to deliver a message about the dangers of nuclear weapons. For example, Dr. Serizawa explains his reluctance to use his Oxygen Destroyer. He fears the "politicians of the world" will take his design and produce many more of the weapon. Dr. Serizawa does not want to contribute to violence around the world. He does not want to "add another terrifying weapon to the arsenal." In a moving scene at the end of the movie, Dr. Yamane solemnly declares, "If nuclear testing continues, then someday, somewhere in the world another Gojira may appear."

Honda knew he was making a monster movie, and *Gojira* has all the action-packed excitement of a good one. To get his larger points across, Honda directed the film in a documentary-like style. Scenes of army troops marching in, navy fleets sailing out, panicked crowds and frantic evacuations, and most of all, wide shots of

Tokyo in flames, all have a realistic quality to them. Honda deliberately balanced the thrills of battling a prehistoric monster with serious thoughts about the post–World War II era. He also felt monster movies "are the most visual kind of film."

Eiji Tsuburaya had the tough job of creating a monster that would live up to this idea.

Eiji Tsuburaya

The Japanese word *tokusatsu* (say: toe-ku-sa-zoo) roughly translates to "special filming." Eiji Tsuburaya is considered the first *tokusatsu* master of Japan. For *Gojira*, he used a combination of miniature sets, puppets, special photography tricks, and his pioneering technique, the monster "suit."

Action! Japanese Style

Tokusatsu is used to describe live-action films or television shows that rely heavily on special effects and often feature actors in costumes. This form of entertainment is very popular in modern Japan, but it comes out of historical Japanese theater. The special effects in these classical

performances might include elaborate makeup, complicated fight scenes, or puppets.

The Godzilla movies are important examples of *tokusatsu*. They even have their own special category. *Tokusatsu* films or shows that feature large monsters like Godzilla are called *kaiju* (say: KAI-joo). This word originally referred to fantastic creatures from Japanese folktales and legends.

Tsuburaya and his team built their own Tokyo for Gojira to stomp through. Their mini movie set included hundreds of downtown city buildings made of plaster, wood, chalk, and glass. Many of them were recognizable landmarks, even

though they were only one twenty-fifth the size of the real structures. It was the first time such a very small set had been used to show the destruction of an entire city in a movie.

The special effects scenes were directed by

Tsuburaya. He placed cameras at low angles. This made buildings appear taller and Gojira look towering. He filmed at speeds faster than usual, which had an opposite effect. The huge monster seemed to move in slow motion, which made it look even scarier. Special animation techniques were used to make Gojira's dorsal fins glow down its spine and the heat ray blast out of its mouth. And then there was *the suit*.

Haruo Nakajima

Time and budget meant Tsuburaya had to be really creative when it came to the movie's main character. Gojira, the terror of Tokyo, was actually an actor in a suit!

Tsuburaya developed the special effect "suitmation." An actor climbed into a Gojira "suit" (costume) and was then filmed walking through the tiny sets. This was not as easy as it sounds!

The weather was warm and humid during

the 1954 film shoot. The monster suit was made of wire mesh, bamboo, fabric, and rubber. It weighed about 150 pounds! It was hot (up to 140 degrees) and uncomfortable inside the suit. The actor could only wear it for short periods of time: *very short*, as in only a few minutes. The crew poured sweat out of the Gojira suit during breaks in the filming. Eventually, designers ran a hose through the beast's tail to its neck. Oxygen was pumped in so the actor could breathe better.

The Men in the Heavy Suit

Haruo Nakajima was a veteran actor of war and samurai (Japanese warrior) films. Katsumi Tezuka was a Japanese actor and professional baseball player. They were both also Godzilla.

Stunt actors Nakajima and Tezuka each wore the heavy monster suit in the 1954 original film. After Tezuka tripped into the set, smashing a few buildings—which was *not* in the script—Nakajima spent the most time suited up as Gojira. On top of all the hazards of the suit, Nakajima had to figure out how to move realistically as a giant prehistoric beast that no one had ever seen before. He studied the movements of elephants and bears in a zoo to prepare for the role.

Katsumi Tezuka

The scenes of *Gojira* underwater were shot with an aquarium full of fish placed between the camera and the actor in the creature suit. Hand puppets of Gojira's head and eyes were used in scenes where suitmation wasn't practical or a close-up was more effective. The bottom part of the first Gojira suit—which was too heavy to use—was cut off. Rope suspenders were attached and this outfit was used to show Gojira's giant feet and legs stomping through some scenes.

Ishiro Honda and Eiji Tsuburaya worked hard together. They had to seamlessly combine live-action filming, suitmation scenes, and the other special effects. But the movie still needed one more important thing: a soundtrack.

Japanese composer Akira Ifukube was not given much time to create the music and sound effects for *Gojira*. He did not even get to see the film before he started composing! Still, he composed memorable music that has lived on.

Akira Ifukube

Selections of Ifukube's music from the first movie have been used in other Godzilla films.

And he created one of the most famous sounds in movie history.

Gojira's roar actually came from rubbing a leather glove covered in resin (plant sap) up and down the strings of a double bass. This string instrument has very low tones. The recorded sound was then played back at a lower speed.

Now, decades later, when audiences hear that
threatening cry they know it can only come from
one thing: Godzilla.

CHAPTER 4
Headed to America

Gojira opened in Tokyo on November 3, 1954. Long lines of people headed into the theater to see the movie. Many were in tears on their way out. They were stirred by scenes so similar to wartime destruction and by the warning messages about the nuclear age. Some people even felt sorry for the creature whose anger was caused by humans interfering with nature. The original movie was a much more serious experience for Japanese audiences than it would prove to be for Americans.

Poster for original 1954 *Gojira* film

There had been very limited screenings of the original 1954 *Gojira* in the United States, mostly in cities with Japanese communities. When it landed in America in wide release two years later, *Gojira* had become *Godzilla, King of the Monsters!* More than its name had changed, though.

The 1956 "Americanization" of *Gojira* included dubbing, or adding a new soundtrack in English, rather than in Japanese. Since it wasn't that long ago that Japan and the United States had been at war with each other, parts of the original film were considered to be sensitive for some audiences. Not all of the original dialogue was translated. Some scenes were deleted or changed to shift the tone of the movie. Dr. Yamane's last line was also rewritten.

About twenty minutes of the original *Gojira* film were edited out. What was edited *in* was Canadian-American actor Raymond Burr. Foreign films were not familiar or popular in the United States in the 1950s. The producers felt American moviegoers at the time would need to see a white person in a lead role. Burr became the central narrator of *Godzilla, King of the Monsters!*

Burr plays Steve Martin, an American

Raymond Burr

journalist in Tokyo when Godzilla stomps into town. The story in the 1956 film is told from Martin's point of view. It was a tricky job to write, shoot, and edit this new character into the existing *Gojira* footage and story. So the American filmmakers rearranged some of the original movie. Their new version started and ended with Steve Martin. Dialogue was added so that Martin sounded like he was on location, reporting what Godzilla was doing. New scenes were shot and inserted into the existing movie. To do this, actor Raymond Burr was sometimes filmed from behind or in scenes with stand-ins. When this footage was edited in, it looked like the character of Steve Martin was interacting with the original Japanese movie characters.

Raymond Burr, playing Steve Martin, also had the last word in the film. Instead of Dr. Yamane's dark warning about the future dangers of nuclear testing, *Godzilla, King of the Monsters!* ends on more of an upbeat, "problem solved" note. Steve Martin concludes, "The whole world could wake up and live again."

Toho sold the American film rights to the American producers, Jewell Enterprises, for $25,000. The companies then worked together. Toho provided original footage and Jewell Enterprises produced what was needed for the Americanization. *Godzilla, King of the Monsters!* opened on April 4, 1956, in New York City and about three weeks later in theaters across the United States. While some movie critics didn't like it, American audiences went all in for Godzilla. The movie was the first made-in-Japan film that was successful in the United States. From there, *Godzilla, King of the Monsters!* went international. It was even released in Japan in 1957. The reedited film was a hit with Japanese audiences.

Godzilla may have died at the end of the original movie, but its story didn't end there. This monster had many movie lives ahead of it!

CHAPTER 5
Emperor Eras

Godzilla appears in more than thirty Toho films. Because there are so many of these monster movies, they are often organized into different eras. The first two eras are named after the reigns of Japanese emperors. Showa Godzilla films were made between 1954 and 1975, during the Showa (meaning "enlightened harmony") rule of Emperor Hirohito. His son, Akihito, was emperor during most of the Heisei (meaning "become peace") period. Heisei Era Godzilla movies span roughly 1984 to 1995.

The Showa Era films include the 1954 *Gojira*, as well as movies that introduced some of the other "Big Five" monsters of the Toho moviemaking world.

Showa Era

After the success of *Gojira*, Toho immediately produced a sequel, *Godzilla Raids Again*. Like the original film, bomb testing was part of the backstory. However, the 1955 movie also introduced an idea that was very new at the time: a plot that centered around two gigantic monsters bashing it out. (The second monster in this film is Anguirus, a dinosaur-like creature with horns and spikes who can move very fast and even leap.) This formula of "Godzilla vs . . ." would prove to be very influential—and popular!

Anguirus

People flocked to see this sequel. Then they had to wait seven years before Toho brought Godzilla back to life on the big screen. The studio was producing other science-fiction movies. But building a whole series about one monster was still an untested idea at the time.

Toho eventually matched their famous *kaiju* with an equally famous ape in *King Kong vs. Godzilla* (1962). In this movie, a businessman captures King Kong and brings it to Japan to be his company's mascot. Meanwhile, an American submarine accidently frees Godzilla, who is trapped in an iceberg. It heads to Japan, of course.

Toho's Big Five

Godzilla is the first of Toho's "Big Five." These *kaiju* monsters appear in the Toho Godzilla movies of every era.

MOTHRA: A massive mutant moth, often accompanied by twin female fairies. Their songs summon and guide the giant fuzzy insect. Mothra is Toho's first female creature. This "Queen of the Monsters" can create hurricane winds by beating her wings. She can also shoot laser beams from her antennae.

KING GHIDORAH: A golden flying dragon that uses its three ferocious heads to blast out high-voltage gravity beams. It lifts up or upends enemies with these powerful, hot beams. It also wraps its necks around enemies to choke them and on rare occasions has fired lightning from its wings.

RODAN: This soaring monster was inspired by *Pteranodon*, a winged dinosaur. It levels buildings by generating a sonic boom with its wide wings.

MECHAGODZILLA: This mechanical monster was created by space aliens. It looks like Godzilla in a suit of armor. It launches missiles from its fingers, toes, even its metal knees!

In the movie universe, the Big Five can be allies or enemies. But in the end, Godzilla always shows them—and the world—who's King of the Monsters!

This monster mash-up was the first time either of the creatures had appeared in a color film. Suitmation was used again. Godzilla got a brand-new costume. The King Kong ape suit was not the least bit authentic, but audiences loved it. The movie was a huge box-office hit. (Spoiler alert: King Kong wins and then swims home.)

Toho saw how responsive people were to Godzilla and how much they liked monsters battling each other. The movies kept coming.

In 1964, Godzilla tangled with Mothra and then with Ghidorah (the dragon didn't become "King" until a later movie). Many fans consider the early Showa films the "Golden Age" of Godzilla movies. They are classic science-fiction monster movies with a message that was often about disturbing nature or the impact of the atomic age, something many people in the world were still getting used to. This "message" approach began to change in the later Showa period.

Movies in general began to face more competition from television. TV was fairly new at the time, but it grew very rapidly. As television expanded its share of the entertainment business, Toho's movie budgets shrank. This impacted the quality of the Godzilla films of the late Showa Era. Toho decided to try to expand its audiences for Godzilla movies.

Increasingly, the movies were directed at young people and children. Godzilla and other monster characters were often funny rather than frightening. *Son of Godzilla* (1967) introduces Minilla (sometimes called Minya), a goofy infant Godzilla who blows smoke rings.

Minilla

In *All Monsters Attack* (1969), Godzilla shows Minilla how to stand up to a bully. These scenes are really the dreams of a lonely child who's being bullied himself. Through the dream sequences, Godzilla helps the boy. Another little boy is a main character in *Godzilla vs. Megalon* (1973). In fact, the robot that helps save the day in this movie was based on a drawing submitted to a Toho contest by an elementary school student.

While the late Showa films often took a more lighthearted approach to Godzilla, the last movie of the era was more intense. In the complicated plot of *Terror of Mechagodzilla* (1975), Godzilla works with Interpol (the international police) to defeat a mad scientist, a sea monster, aliens, and robots. After that, it seemed like moviegoers had tired of monsters. Godzilla disappeared from movie screens for nine years.

Like *Gojira*, some of Toho's other Showa Era Godzilla films were edited, dubbed into English, and distributed in the United States. Also like *Gojira*, films for the American market usually got new titles and often lost some of their political messages. Japanese audiences recognized deeper meanings or serious content when it was part of Godzilla movies. In the Americanized versions, the movies were usually considered "B" movies.

These low-budget, less serious films were shown before the main attraction of a double feature. The Americanized Godzilla movies also ran on US television stations that showed "creature features," programming of monster and science-fiction movies. And they were sometimes available as home videos, a popular media at the time.

CHAPTER 6
Big, Bad, and Back

In the Heisei Era, Toho decided to reboot the Godzilla franchise. Now Godzilla was big, bad, and back as a super menace!

Most of the Godzilla films of this period were not widely available in the United States. Toho's main monster faced stiff competition from American filmmakers. Blockbusters like the Star Wars and Indiana Jones series had taken special effects to a new level. These Hollywood movies made the Godzilla movies look old-fashioned to many people. Still, Heisei Godzilla brought plenty of viewers into theaters in Japan, and even inspired some scientists!

Tomoyuki Tanaka, the producer of the original *Gojira* movie, worked hard to convince

Special effects

Toho to bring back the earlier, powerful version of its giant beast. Godzilla returned to being its terrorizing, destructive old self. There was more continuity (connected action or details) from one plot to another in the Heisei movies. Sometimes characters reappeared from movie to movie. Heisei Godzilla films had plenty of crowd-pleasing monster clashes. But the plots of these movies were based on modern concerns about global threats, pollution, and science experiments. The movies from this era also featured many military scenes and all kinds of technology. This mirrored Japan's real growth as a world power.

The first film of the Heisei Era was *The Return of Godzilla*. (In Japan, it was known as *Gojira*.) Released in December 1984, the movie is an action-packed, direct sequel of the original *Gojira*.

For Real?

Watching the original Godzilla movie as a child wowed Japanese-American Kenneth Carpenter. It also inspired what became his life's work: paleontology. In 1997, Carpenter honored the influential monster. He officially described and named a real dinosaur *Gojirasaurus quayi*.

Gojirasaurus came from the Japanese name for Godzilla; *quayi* is because the dinosaur fossils were discovered in the Copper Canyon Formation in Quay County, New Mexico. Like Godzilla, this dinosaur is thought to have been very large: perhaps eighteen feet long, possibly weighing four hundred pounds or more. Meat-eating *Gojirasaurus quayi* lived 228 to 208 million years ago. Now its few fossils rest at the University of Colorado, Boulder.

Scientists still debate whether the fossils have been correctly classified or whether some may belong to other dinosaurs. Even this would be Godzilla-like: The movie-star monster is a mash-up of different dinosaur types such as *T. rex*, stegosaurus, and iguanodon.

Godzilla is again creating massive disruption and almost brings about a nuclear war! Like the

original 1954 film, *The Return of Godzilla* was Americanized. English-language scenes with actor Raymond Burr were added. The film was reedited and renamed Godzilla 1985. But it didn't really take off with American audiences.

While Godzilla remained a familiar character, it faced some strange new foes in a few of the Heisei films. In *Godzilla vs. Biollante* (1989), the Big G takes on a towering plant! Biollante is a genetic experiment gone wrong. This monster is created from the cells of a dead young woman, a flower, and Godzilla itself. Now it's reptile vs. rose! Godzilla is attacked by the giant, weeping flower monster with long, choking stems and sharp-toothed buds. Meanwhile, Japanese scientists try to keep their experiments out of the hands of Middle Eastern and American secret agents.

Biollante

In *Godzilla vs. SpaceGodzilla* (1994), the original monster has to fight its own clone! SpaceGodzilla is created when the Big G's cells were zapped by radiation from a black hole in space. Of course, SpaceGodzilla heads right to Earth to start trouble.

Godzilla faces off against SpaceGodzilla

In between these quirky films, Toho produced a couple of other movies where Godzilla faces popular older rivals like King Ghidorah, Mothra, and Mechagodzilla.

Then, in *Godzilla vs. Destoroyah* (1995), Godzilla's fearsome opponent comes right out of the ending of the original movie. When the Oxygen Destroyer killed off Gojira, pieces of it fell to the ocean floor and turned small, fossilized extinct marine animals into human-size monsters. Even worse, the six-legged creatures merge, grow wings, and become an even bigger single creature called Destoroyah.

Destoroyah

The final battle is on! In this fight, Godzilla has absorbed so much energy that its huge heart undergoes a meltdown. As the giant beast throws up its head, roars, and melts away, a chorus sings a mournful melody written by the original movie's composer, Akira Ifukube. Godzilla is no more.

The Heisei Era films helped restore Godzilla to its rightful place with movie fans, though mainly in Japan. Most of the Heisei Godzilla films didn't make it to America. But Godzilla still had a big impact on Hollywood moviemakers.

Steven Spielberg

Steven Spielberg has said that his blockbuster *Jurassic Park* (1993), based on a Michael Crichton novel, was inspired by the Japanese monster: "Godzilla was the most masterful of all dinosaur movies because it made you believe it was really happening."

CHAPTER 7
Millennium Era Onward

Even before they'd killed off their monster, Toho agreed to a license with the movie company Sony/TriStar. This studio would create the first original American Godzilla movie. Their *Godzilla* (1998) was a financial success, but did not receive a warm welcome from fans. Many of them thought the Sony/TriStar Godzilla

looked more like a dinosaur from *Jurassic Park* than the classic creature from Japan. They felt the movie didn't have the popular appeal of the Toho G-films.

When the 1998 Sony/TriStar film did not capture what fans and moviegoers felt was the essential Godzilla, Toho started to plan for the future. The studio reclaimed the rights to Godzilla and got ready for another reboot (a new start to an existing series). This third round of Toho films is called the Millennium Era, which spans 1999 to 2004, the years surrounding the dawning of the new millennium in the year 2000. Like the Showa and Heisei eras, this era has its own characteristics. It is also the shortest of the Toho eras.

Poster for *Godzilla 2000*

Does Size Matter?

In 1998, you couldn't escape the slogan "Size Does Matter." It was on billboards all across the United States. Sometimes a giant clawed foot stood beneath the headline. Other times, an enormous red eye glared out above the words.

Sony/TriStar ramped up people's curiosity even more by not releasing any images of their monster before *Godzilla* opened across the country on May 20, 1998.

Some fans thought the marketing of *Godzilla* was better than the movie itself! Some critics called the movie "GINO": Godzilla in Name Only.

Millennium Godzilla movies are very action-oriented. The more monster bashing, crashing, and smashing, the better! For the most part, they were written to be standalone movies, not as part of a series. Unlike the Heisei Era films, their plots do not usually build on the stories of earlier Godzilla movies or depend on any single timeline. Toho also hired different directors for the various Millennium Era films. Each director brought his own individual style to the moviemaking.

Orga

Godzilla remains a stomping, fire-breathing natural disaster in the six Toho films of this period. There are battles with some new enemies, like the freaky-faced Orga in *Godzilla 2000* (released in 1999). This ancient alien partially swallows Godzilla, only to be blasted apart from the inside by Big G's fiery heat ray.

Godzilla vs. Megaguirus (2000) has a complicated plot that involves black holes and giant prehistoric dragonfly monsters. Godzilla's robotic counterpart is back and ready to rumble in *Godzilla Against Mechagodzilla* (2002). Meanwhile, Japan's capital

Megaguirus

city gets flattened again in *Godzilla: Tokyo S.O.S.* (2003). The ever-popular Mothra flies in to join the fight, too.

Godzilla, Mothra, and King Ghidorah: Giant Monsters All-Out Attack (2001) has the longest title of all the Millennium Era movies and is often rated the most interesting one of this era. The story begins with the idea that the souls of some people who died in the Pacific battles of World War II have become part of Godzilla. These spirits urge the Big G to destroy Japan. "Guardian Monsters," including Mothra and King Ghidorah, come to the rescue.

Eventually, Godzilla is defeated, explodes, and sinks into the sea. His heart falls to the ocean floor . . . and keeps beating!

Toho released *Godzilla: Final Wars* (2004) at the fiftieth anniversary of the Godzilla franchise.

Everything gets thrown into this movie along with Godzilla: superhuman mutant soldiers, aliens arriving by spaceship, a planet about to collide with Earth, Godzilla's son Minilla, and plenty of *kaiju*, from Rodan to Anguirus to Mothra (once again!).

Toho's Millennium Era Godzilla movies had to compete with the blockbuster movies coming to Japan from the United States. Moviegoers' expectations had changed with the times. And by the early twenty-first century, computer-generated imagery (CGI) was used extensively in moviemaking. The audience began to lose interest in Godzilla, and it showed at the box office.

The King of the Monsters was having a hard time keeping up with the king of moviemaking: Hollywood.

What's a Monster to Wear?

Godzilla continued to be a man in a monster suit in the Heisei Era through the Millennium Era films. Over the decades, the look of these Godzilla suits changed. Heads and tails were resized and reused. Dorsal fins were added or subtracted. Body proportions were sometimes bulky, sometimes sleek. Eyes moved or just stared wide open or even glowed. Tiny ears came and went. Different Godzilla suits were different colors, ranging from brown to charcoal gray to dark green to light green.

Parts were recycled from one movie's monster suit to the next. Materials also changed over time, in order to make the monster costume more flexible. Suitmation peaked with *Godzilla: Final Wars.* By that time, the Godzilla suit was lighter by about forty-four pounds.

Many of the Godzilla costumes, including the original 1954 Gojira suit, simply rotted away or wore out from heavy use. (Although one 1991 Godzilla suit made headlines when it was *stolen*! Luckily, it was found abandoned on a beach. Its recovery made for some great news photos!)

However, Toho does have a 1994 Godzilla costume, along with other monster suits from the Millennium Era, preserved in temperature-controlled storage in their Tokyo studios.

CHAPTER 8
High Tech in Hollywood *and* Tokyo

On November 29, 2004, around the fiftieth anniversary of the original movie, Godzilla made headlines in the United States. The monster got its own star for "achievements in film" alongside all the other notable names on the Hollywood Walk of Fame in California. It seemed as if the monster's actual star power was fading after Toho's Millennium Era films. But the next decade would bring the King of the Monsters back to the world's attention!

Hollywood's Legendary Pictures studio reached an agreement with Toho to bring out American Godzilla movies once again. Mothra, King Ghidorah, and Rodan also joined King Kong in Legendary's MonsterVerse.

The MonsterVerse films share important concepts that are developed within the individual movie plots. The main ideas are Monarch and Massive Unidentified Terrestrial Organisms (MUTOs). Monarch is a secret international scientific and government agency. Its agents are studying and trying to contain whatever MUTOs appear and threaten humanity.

The MUTOs have radioactive origins or characteristics. Monarch's research also reveals the presence of "Titans," monsters like Godzilla. The Titans were once considered gods that coexisted with human beings. However, people's disrespect for the environment and disregard for the impact of nuclear testing upset the balance of nature. As a result, the MUTOs and Titans are mad. And they are on the move! This is the structure for Legendary's MonsterVerse—and Godzilla is at the center of that movie universe.

Legendary's first film in the franchise is *Godzilla* (2014). It opens with chilling scenes of a nuclear power plant meltdown in Japan. An American scientist working there loses his wife in the accident. He spends his life trying to prove this was not a natural disaster. He is right: The meltdown was caused by MUTO activity. Even worse, Monarch is hiding a MUTO in the ruined power plant. That MUTO hatches into an enormous flying insect that likes to eat radioactive material, especially nuclear warheads (explosive missiles). It's not alone, either: Its even bigger MUTO mate hatches in Nevada and immediately demolishes the city of Las Vegas.

Off the coast of Honolulu, Hawaii, Godzilla is disturbed by the MUTOs' signals to each other. It arises to fight the giant insect monsters, setting up a tsunami that floods the city.

Finally, it is the moment the audience has been waiting for: the first appearance of Godzilla. Flares shoot into a dark sky and continue going up, up, up, illuminating what looks like a scaly *wall* of monster! This Godzilla is so big you can't even fully see it on the screen. But you can hear its famous roar!

This partial-view technique is used effectively throughout the movie, when the audience sees only parts of the monster. Suddenly a spiked spine emerges from the water, headed straight for an aircraft carrier. A long, powerful tail crashes down between dark city skyscrapers and disappears. A boom shakes the floor-to-ceiling windows of a building as a huge foot stomps by. A giant clawed hand tears at the suspensions of a bridge crowded with vehicles and trapped people. The effects are heightened by the film's often dark and smoky look.

The *Godzilla* story follows the scientist and

his son, a naval officer, who uncover Monarch's MUTO conspiracy in Japan. Meanwhile, the son's wife and child are back home in San Francisco, where Godzilla and the enormous insect MUTOs eventually meet. While the monsters rampage, the US military sends in a warhead to stop them. The MUTOs stop this plan by stealing the warhead from a train. Now there is both a dangerous bomb countdown *and* gigantic creatures to deal with!

The naval officer helps save the day and send the bomb out to sea to explode. Godzilla also triumphs. It destroys the MUTOs—and much of San Francisco in the process—and then collapses. Just as people realize Godzilla actually saved them, the Big G awakens and lumbers back into the sea.

While Legendary was busy in Hollywood with its MonsterVerse, after a twelve-year gap, Toho returned to the monster it created.

Godzilla is scary enough, but imagine if the gigantic beast could shapeshift! That's exactly what happens in *Shin Godzilla*, Toho's 2016 epic and the first Toho Godzilla film to rely on CGI instead of suitmation.

Shin Godzilla's standalone storyline does not connect to other Godzilla movies. In fact, this Godzilla is an entirely new species, energized by nuclear waste. The movie plot veers from monster mayhem to military maneuvers to messy politics. There is a huge cast and thousands of extras. But the undisputed star is Godzilla, who can change its size and shape. The Big G morphs from underwater terror to unstoppable threat on land. When the monster is attacked, *it evolves*. First seen, it looks like a super-large, menacing serpent tail. Then it's a big, creepy, eel-like thing with unblinking eyes, wriggling through Tokyo's streets, wrecking everything. But it's Shin Godzilla, towering upright and walking on two legs, that's really frightening. Its skin glows burning red hot from within. Its tail is in constant, sweeping, destructive motion. It belches its famous fiery breath *and* blasts purple heat-ray lasers all along its spine and out its tail.

Plus each mutated Godzilla form is bigger and more indestructible than the last!

Shin Godzilla takes a unique and intense new approach to its celebrated creature. It was also widely seen as a significant comment on Japanese bureaucracy, contemporary environmental issues, and international relations, especially between Japan and the United States. The popular Toho movie was released in Japan on July 29, 2016. It became the top-earning movie in Japan that year and won seven Japan Academy Prizes, including Picture, Director, and Art Direction of the Year awards. In October 2016, it was released in the United States as *Shin Godzilla*.

Three years later, Legendary released *Godzilla: King of the Monsters* (2019).

Now the Titans include Hollywood versions of the classic Toho characters, Mothra, Rodan, and King Ghidorah. In this movie, a Monarch scientist invents a sound device by which she thinks she can control the Titans. She's wrong. The scientist, her daughter, and the device are all then captured by terrorists who free the fierce Titan King Ghidorah. Being *the only* monster king is definitely Ghidorah's plan.

The vicious three-headed dragon calls its many fellow Titans to awaken, arise, and destroy the world. There is only one creature on Earth that can stop them: Godzilla! Monarch scientists and the world's military leaders detonate a nuclear warhead to revive Godzilla in his underwater lair just in time. And luckily, Mothra emerges from her cocoon to help out.

Godzilla Stats

- **HEIGHT:** varies, from 165 to 394 feet (as buildings in the real world rose higher and higher, Godzilla in the movie world had to grow taller, too)
- **WEIGHT:** 164,000 tons (an estimate from *Popular Mechanics* science writers)
- **FEET:** sometimes three-toed, sometimes four-toed, always extra, extra, extra large
- **SPECIAL FEATURES:** ear-splitting roar, deadly heat ray, glowing spinal plates
- **LIKES:** swimming, stomping, setting fires, smackdowns
- **DISLIKES:** other monsters, fighter planes, tanks, battleships, armies, navies, and bridges and buildings in its path
- **REALLY DISLIKES:** being awakened by bomb tests; people and monsters disturbing nature
- **REALLY LIKES:** being left alone

The Titans are lured to Fenway Park, home of the Boston Red Sox. King Ghidorah comes after them and Godzilla comes after the evil dragon. By this time, every part of Godzilla is bursting with energy. Its very skin is glowing red!

The big, violent showdowns begin. Godzilla repeatedly blasts King Ghidorah. The dragon fights hard but loses two of its heads. Godzilla bites off the third one and swallows it. Ghidorah is dead. As the human characters in the story watch from a plane, Godzilla stands tall atop the ruins of the city of Boston.

The other Titans surround the victor and bow down to the King of the Monsters. Godzilla roars triumphantly! The movie's credits include a teaser: ancient cave paintings that show Godzilla fighting with a very familiar figure—Kong!

And that's exactly where Legendary goes next.

Godzilla vs. Kong (2021) is a rematch nearly sixty years after the original giant ape/giant dino dustup. As one character in the film says, "These are dangerous times." The movie has a complicated story. The action is set in many places, including Kong's home on Skull Island, "Hollow Earth"—the kingdom of the Titans inside the planet—and Hong Kong, for the big battle scene. Godzilla and Kong are causing major damage . . . until Mechagodzilla shows up. In a thrilling ending, the two monsters join forces to defeat the robot. But Godzilla and Kong are an uneasy team. There's still enough of a feud between them to keep audiences eagerly awaiting their next encounter in Legendary's 2024 MonsterVerse movie *Godzilla x Kong: The New Empire.*

Legendary's filmmakers worked hard to keep the things that fans of the Toho movies liked. Their Godzilla looked and sounded like a pumped-up version of the original beast. (The studio once tested their Godzilla roar and it could be heard three miles away!) Many shots in the Legendary films show Godzilla in comparison to the human actors in the scene. This gives audiences a "you-are-there" sense of scale.

Seventy years into the franchise, CGI has replaced the man-in-the-monster suit, the creatures are bigger and scarier than ever, and the movies are released internationally. But Godzilla remains, as always, the King of the Monsters!

CHAPTER 9
Living Legend

Godzilla has appeared in dozens of movies and has even died in four of them. But the giant beast remains a living legend. There are Godzilla cartoons, as well as a live-action Godzilla series developed by Toho, Legendary, and Apple TV+. The episodes follow a family trying to figure out its connections to Monarch. They're also navigating their way through the world of Titans, where myths and monsters are real—and dangerous.

Godzilla is resurrected again and again and always finds an audience happy to see it. That may be because, from the start, Godzilla movies have kept current with the times in which they are made. In addition to special effects and action-packed excitement, they deal with ideas and issues from the real world like nuclear fears, environmental disasters, and the uses and misuses of science. They also feature a monster character that viewers often support even as they cheer on its destruction. Or to quote one of the movies, "This is Godzilla's world, we just live in it."

In between movies, Godzilla lovers can still immerse themselves in their favorite monster's world. After the daring ride on the zipline at Nijigen no Mori Park, fans can visit the Godzilla museum there, play a game to destroy Godzilla's radioactive cells, eat Godzilla curry, and drink a Godzilla fruit punch.

Stay-at-home types can open up the Godzilla Monopoly board and choose their playing pieces: Godzilla, Mothra, Rodan, King Ghidorah, Mechagodzilla, and Minilla. Or fill in the blanks with other words for fear and destruction with *Godzilla Mad Libs*.

Heads Up!

Although Godzilla destroyed Tokyo several times over, the Japanese city still celebrates its world-famous monster.

In Hibiya Godzilla Square, it's honored with a ten-foot statue and a sign, "The human race must coexist with Godzilla," a quote from Toho's *Shin Godzilla.*

Godzilla is officially a tourism ambassador and resident of Tokyo's Shinjuku area. A forty-foot, eighty-ton sculpture of its head watches over the district from atop the Toho skyscraper. Occasionally, this monster's eyes glow and it roars and belches smoke. Lucky guests at the Hotel Gracery get a close-up on this giant head. Or they can book the "Godzilla Room," where a life-size monster claw breaks through the hotel wall right above the bed.

There are trivia books, coloring books, and comic books based on the Godzilla legend. Some colleges offer courses that explore the history of Godzilla and other monsters in Japanese culture. Of course, a creature as popular as Godzilla has been reproduced in a wide variety of merchandise, including posters, action figures, giant inflatables, and even pajamas.

Toho has an office in Los Angeles, California, responsible for preserving Godzilla's reputation by keeping track of how the Godzilla image is used. Godzilla has its own official website and social media channels, including YouTube, Instagram, and X/Twitter. Enthusiastic G-fans also maintain websites and hold G-Fest conventions, though all of that is unofficial.

Many of the earlier Godzilla movies can now

be streamed, reaching a wider audience than ever. This means more and more people can fully understand and appreciate Godzilla's history, significance, and impact. That's only fitting for a creature that stars in the longest-running film franchise in history.

All hail, Godzilla, King of the Monsters!

Bibliography

*Books for young readers

*Beccia, Carlyn. *Monstrous: The Lore, Gore, and Science Behind Your Favorite Monsters*. Minneapolis, MN: Carolrhoda Books, 2019.

*Burnham, Erik, and Dan Schoening. *Godzilla: Monsters & Protectors, Rise Up!* San Diego, CA: IDW Publishing, 2022.

Edwards, Gareth, director. *Godzilla*. 2014; Hollywood, CA: Legendary Pictures, Warner Brothers.

Failes, Ian. "The History of Godzilla Is the History of Special Effects," *Inverse*. October 14, 2016. www.inverse.com/article/22234-special-effects-in-godzilla-movies-history.

Honda, Ishiro, director. *Gojira*. 1954; Tokyo, Japan: Toho Co., Ltd, Jewell Enterprises.

Honda, Ishiro, and Terry O. Morse, directors. *Godzilla, King of the Monsters!* 1956; Tokyo, Japan: Toho Co., Ltd.

Honda, Ishiro, and Motoyoshi Oda, directors. *Godzilla Raids Again*. 1955; Tokyo, Japan: Toho Co., Ltd.

LIFE (editors). *Godzilla: The King of the Monsters*. New York: Meredith Corporation, 2019.

*Macchiarola, Laura. *Godzilla Mad Libs*. New York: Mad Libs, 2021.

National Museum of Nuclear Science & History. "Gojira (1954)."
American Heritage Foundation. November 14, 2018. https://
ahf.nuclearmuseum.org/ahf/history/gojira-1954/.

Skipper, Graham. *Godzilla: The Ultimate Illustrated Guide*.
London: Welbeck Publishing, 2022.

Solomon, Brian. *Godzilla FAQ: All That's Left to Know About
the King of the Monsters*. Lanham, MD: Applause Theatre &
Cinema Books, 2017.

Wingard, Adam, director. *Godzilla vs. Kong*. 2021; Hollywood,
CA: Legendary Pictures, Warner Brothers.

Websites

Instagram: godzilla_toho

www.criterion.com/search#stq=Godzilla

www.godzilla.com

www.legendary.com

www.toho.co.jp/en/company/info/history

X/Twitter: @GODZILLA_TOHO